2/23/80

They Found a Way

Lorraine Hansberry

By Catherine Scheader

Campus Publications

CHILDRENS PRESS, CHICAGO

TO BARBARA, JOHN, AND SUSAN

ACKNOWLEDGMENTS

The author is grateful to Mamie Hansberry Mitchell, who shared her memories of her sister and of her remarkable parents and her brothers.

My appreciation is extended to Shauneille Perry, Miss Hansberry's cousin, who despite her own professional and family commitments, took the time to answer questions and to write to me identifying and describing family members and her memories of family celebrations in her childhood.

I wish to thank Robert Nemiroff, who as Miss Hansberry's literary executor, was generous in making available manuscript material and copies of interviews with the late playwright. Mr. Nemiroff consented to hours of interviews about Miss Hansberry's life in New York, and clarified details about the productions of her plays. Both he and Mrs. Mitchell were kind enough to read a draft of the manuscript of this book and offer suggestions and corrections. In addition, Mr. Nemiroff provided access to the photographic material used in this book.

Finally, I am grateful to Mary Mainzer and Susan Scheader, who represented the readership for whom this book was intended, by previewing and reacting to it.

PICTURE CREDITS

Cover painting of Lorraine Hansberry by Gladys Schwarz, photo by Michael Frost; posters on pages 60, 70, 72, 75, and 79 designed by Stan Phillips, photography by Michael Frost; photo on page 52 by Michael Frost; pages 2 and 43, Nat Fein, *New York Herald Tribune;* page 14, bottom, Monarch Photo; page 18, Bill Yoscary; page 25, *Amsterdam News;* pages 46 and 48, Gin Briggs; page 60, top right, photograph by Jos. Abeles Studio; page 60, bottom left and right, and page 72, bottom, Friedman Abeles; page 72, top right, Martha Swope; page 79, top right, Rhetta Hughes; page 79, bottom, Bert Andrews Photography.

Library of Congress Cataloging in Publication Data

Scheader, Catherine.
  Lorraine Hansberry.

  (They found a way)
  SUMMARY: A biography of the playwright who was the first black person and the youngest American to receive the best play of the year award.
  1. Hansberry, Lorraine, 1930-1965—Biography—Juvenile literature.
2. Dramatists, American—20th century—Biography—Juvenile literature.
[1. Hansberry, Lorraine, 1930-1965. 2. Dramatists. 3. Afro-Americans—Biography] I. Title. II. Series.
PS3515.A515Z87   812'.5'4 [B] [92]   77-7279
ISBN 0-516-01851-5

Copyright© 1978 by Regensteiner Publishing Enterprises, Inc.
All rights reserved. Printed in the U.S.A.
Published simultaneously in Canada.
1 2 3 4 5 6 7 8 9 10 11 12 R 85 84 83 82 81 80 79 78

CHAPTER ONE

Lorraine sat on the porch rail, her back to the street. Her feet were hooked around the bars and her hands were free.

"Mamie, clap with me!" she cried to her older sister. "Let's do 'Teddy Bear!'"

"Lorraine," groaned Mamie. "I'm too big for that. Do it on the wall."

"No fun!" replied the younger girl, shaking her head vigorously. "Besides, Mama said you should play with me," she added, deliberately teasing.

"She said I should *stay* with you, Lorraine. Honestly, the way you try to get 'round me!"

But Mamie rose from the steps, stood in front of her little sister and clapped hands with her to the rhythm of the old chant that she herself had loved a few years before.

"I had a little teddy bear, his name was Tiny Tim.
I put him in the bathtub to see if he could swim.
He drank all the water, he ate all the soap.
He died the next morning with a bubble in his throat.
In came the doctor, in came the nurse.
In came the lady with the alligator purse.

'Measles,' said the doctor. 'Mumps,' said the nurse.
'Nothing,' said the lady with the alligator purse.
Out walked the doctor, out walked the nurse.
Out walked the lady with the alligator purse.''

Lorraine felt almost happy again. The good thing about moving to this house in the white neighborhood was that Mrs. Hansberry had told her older daughter to keep an eye on Lorraine. If it weren't for Mamie, she would be very lonesome, because it was hard to make friends here. Lorraine missed their old neighborhood and the one good friend she had there.

Although she became accustomed to the curious stares of grown-ups who saw her on the way to school, the jeers and taunts of other children were something else. She tried not to attach any meaning to the words these children were using. Her mother had told her the words had no meaning.

"Kids hear their parents say mean things, and they just repeat them," her mother told her. "They're not thinking about what they're saying. And their words have nothing to do with you, because they don't know you. You are just as good as any of those children. And as smart, too. Just you remember that!"

But it was lonely with no one her age to play with after school. Mamie sometimes fixed her hair and put polish on her nails, but that wasn't fun all the time. The best times were when she went to her cousin Shauneille's for an overnight visit.

Last week her mother had taken her to Shauneille's house. There, with Uncle Graham and Aunt Pearl, everything was like it used to be. She jumped rope and played jacks all day with her

cousin. At night, they whispered and laughed together after the lights were out. If only Shauneille could come to her house this weekend!

Lorraine decided to go right in and ask Mama to invite her over. Mamie had gone back to sitting on the porch steps, gazing across the street. Lorraine slipped down from the porch rail. In a flash, Mamie was at her side. With her hand on Lorraine's arm, she said in a low voice, "Honey, let's go inside. You have homework to do."

"I did my homework, Mamie," the younger girl protested, trying to pull away. Then, aware of the alarm in Mamie's voice, she cried, "What's the matter?"

Mamie did not answer, but tightened her hold on Lorraine's arm as she steered her through the door. Lorraine had time for only a quick look back over her shoulder, but she saw a group of people standing across the street, talking and pointing to their house.

Below: A self-portrait on the cover of Lorraine's grade-school graduation autograph book. Right: Lorraine as a young child.

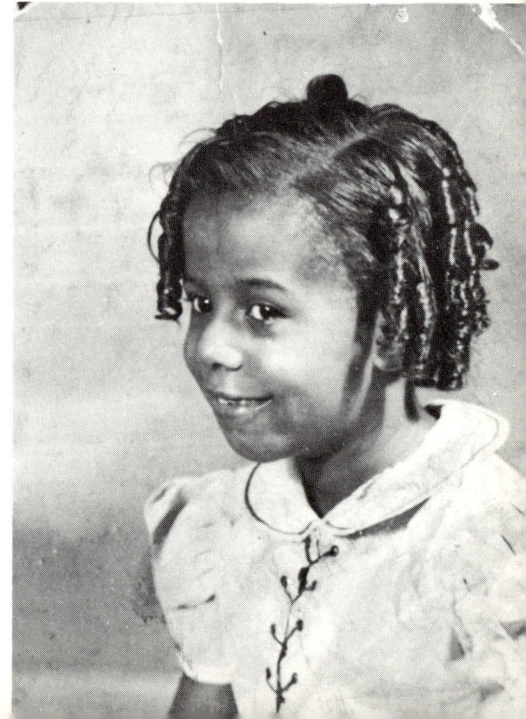

CHAPTER TWO

Inside, Mamie called to her mother.

"It's all right, I see them," her mother answered calmly. "They just came to have a look at us. Carl and Perry will be home soon. You girls stay out of the front room for now."

"Come on, Lorraine. Let's listen to the radio," Mamie said easily, still holding her hand and guiding her into the next room.

Lorraine felt mixed up. She could tell that Mama and Mamie were worried, even though they were trying not to show it.

"Mamie," she began. "I wish Daddy were here. He'd ..."

But her sister would not let her continue. "Lorraine," she insisted, "there's nothing to worry about. Daddy's friend is here, and look—here come Carl and Perry. Mama said they'd be home soon!"

Perry picked her up and spun her around. Lorraine's fear of the crowd outside was forgotten as she shrieked with happy terror from the height. When he finally put her down, she asked, "Perry, where did Daddy go?"

The tall broad-shouldered teen-ager sat down beside her. "Now, you listen to me, and listen carefully," he began very seriously. "Daddy has to be away, Lorraine. He's busy prepar-

ing his court case. You know that we're trying to fight the restrictive covenants of this city."

Restrictive covenants! Those were the big words that grown-ups had talked about for as long as she could remember. Her father, who was a real estate dealer, had told her about the covenants, or agreements, that made Chicago neighborhoods either all black or all white.

"People in a neighborhood can get together and decide that they won't sell any houses to black people," he had explained. "Or rent apartments to them, either. This limits everybody's freedom. If one of the owners wants to sell to a black family, he's not allowed to because of the restrictive covenants.

"Families who come to my real estate office looking for places to live can't move to certain streets, even if there are empty apartments."

One day, not long ago, Mr. Hansberry had heard of a building owner in a white neighborhood who was willing to sell a house to him. If Mr. Hansberry bought the house and a black family occupied it, it would be a clear-cut violation of the restrictive covenant that covered that neighborhood.

There was no question of who that family would be. Daddy and Mama had long, serious talks at the dining room table. Sometimes, friends from downtown came to the house, and they talked together late into the night. They all knew that anyone moving into the house would be breaking the law that protected the restrictive covenants. But the law was unjust, and they were sure it violated the United States Constitution.

Lorraine's mother began to make the moving arrangements at once. Mr. and Mrs. Hansberry were prepared to break the law, and pay whatever penalty they would have to, in order to prove that the law was unconstitutional. Lorraine could tell how serious the decision was, because she kept hearing about the risks involved. Although Lorraine's brothers, Carl and Perry, were glad that Mr. Hansberry was challenging the unfair practice of restricting neighborhoods, Lorraine knew they were worried, too.

But when she asked Perry about it, he said, "Lorraine, sometimes you have to do something you're scared to do, because its *right*."

Lorraine looked carefully at Perry now, wondering whether he was scared.

"Perry," she asked. "Is the court going to help us? Then will Daddy come home? And can we go back to our other house?"

"Slow down, Lorraine," Perry laughed. "Let's take one question at a time!

"First of all, I think the court is going to say that people can live where they want to, no matter what their skin color is. Daddy will come home as soon as his work is finished. Our job is to stay here. We can't let people's words change us. We have a right to be in this house because our father bought it, fair and square, from someone who was willing to sell it to us. We won't give up that right because some other people get nasty about it.

"You having any trouble with those kids in school?" he asked, concerned. "Tell the truth."

"Not really, Perry. I do what Mama said. When they try to start something, I look right at them, and pretend I'm not afraid at all. It works, too!"

"That's my girl," said Perry with a laugh. "And remember what I said. If things get bad, just let me know."

Lorraine smiled up at Perry. She knew that he and Carl would not let anything bad happen to her. That was what big brothers were for.

Suddenly, Perry's smile vanished and his expression became intent. "Shh!" he said sharply, straining to hear some sound in the distance. After a moment, he rose, trying not to make any noise. "Stay here, Lorraine," he whispered. "I'll be right back."

But Lorraine could not resist following her brother out to the front of the house. Everyone was standing in the front room, tense with expectation and facing out toward the street. Lorraine's mother, Mamie, Carl, and Perry were there. So was their maid, and the man introduced to Lorraine as Daddy's friend, but who she knew was really a bodyguard, stationed at home by their father to protect them. Lorraine slipped into a corner, trying not to be noticed.

She could see that the crowd had changed in size and intent. No longer a handful of people staring from across the street, it was now an ugly mob, waving and shouting in anger, and very, very close to the house.

No one inside moved. As the noise and excitement outside grew, those within the room grew quieter and quieter; they

stood rigidly alert. When Lorraine thought she could bear the stillness no longer, it ended explosively in a sudden crash of glass. Something rocketed through the window, whizzed past her, and slammed into the far wall. Instantly, screams and shouts from those inside were mingled with the voices outside. As Lorraine tried to cover her eyes and ears, Carl swept her up in his arms and deposited her, seconds later, in her own room. Mamie rushed in behind him, and huddled beside her, saying over and over, "It's all right, Lorraine. Don't cry."

Lorraine lay on her bed, hands over her ears, sobbing into her pillow. After a time, she must have fallen asleep, because that was all she could remember.

When she awoke, the mob was gone, finally broken up by the bodyguard, who had gone out with a drawn gun. The broken window had been replaced with cardboard and the shattered glass had been cleared away. Someone had removed the object that had lodged in the wall; it lay on a kitchen chair—a piece of concrete the size of a football, possibly torn from a building foundation or a sidewalk.

Left: Lorraine's mother when she arrived from the South. Above: Lorraine's father, Carl Hansberry. Below: The Hansberry's on their twenty-fifth wedding anniversary.

CHAPTER THREE

It was a long time before Lorraine could attach any meaning to that violent day. No one could explain why people did such hateful things. But from that moment, she knew how destructive hatred could be. She understood why her parents urged her to assert her rights.

At first, she thought they would leave the house and the neighborhood, but she was wrong. "We are staying," her father had told her. Friends stopped by more frequently. The black jitney cab drivers from the neighborhood often drove past the house, maintaining a sort of protective vigil. Lorraine realized that people were watching over them.

They probably would not have moved at all if the court case had not gone against them. But it did, and they were ordered to leave the building less than a year later. They moved to Michigan Avenue, and Lorraine transferred from the Sexton School to Betsy Ross, the segregated school, which was on split session.

Lorraine knew that the move was a defeat, and was surprised at her parents' reaction to it. She assumed that since they had lost, that would be the end of it. But she was mistaken. It turned

out that Mr. and Mrs. Hansberry had expected the decision. Mr. Hansberry had already begun to prepare the case for higher courts. Since the restrictive covenants were allowed by law in Illinois, Mr. Hansberry had to show that they violated the United States Constitution. To do this, he had to take his case to a higher court. That was why he had gone to Washington.

"This decision was from an Illinois court, Lorraine. Daddy said he'll take this to the Supreme Court of the United States in Washington, D. C. if he has to," Perry said decisively. "We're all in this till the end," he added proudly.

The end did not come for years. Mr. Hansberry, with the help of the National Association for the Advancement of Colored People (NAACP), ultimately appealed to the United States Supreme Court in 1940. The Supreme Court reversed the Illinois court decision and ruled in his favor. But that was a long time later. In the meantime, much of his time, money, and energy were devoted to the case.

From that early example, Lorraine learned lessons about dedication to a just cause. She decided that if her parents could take such risks for something they believed in, then so could she. From them, she learned early to stand her ground in a dispute.

"When someone gives you trouble," her father said, "hold your head up and look him right in the eye. It's hard for a person to persist in wrongdoing when you do that. Fighting back doesn't always make sense. There are usually too many to fight, and anyway, that makes you just like them. Remember that you

are not like them. You are part of a people with a proud heritage. Our family has been in this country for hundreds of years."

When her father talked about "a proud people," Lorraine thought of Grandmother Perry and the trip the family had made one summer to Columbia, Tennessee to see her. Lorraine's mother had been born in Columbia and many of her relatives, including her mother, still lived there.

The ride to Tennessee, Lorraine recalled, had been hot and dusty. She and her cousin Shauneille sang songs and told riddles to pass the time, and when they grew tired, they slept some. The last time Lorraine had awakened, she had seen the dark, rich hills of Kentucky rising up before her. She shook her cousin's shoulder, "Shauneille, wake up!" she cried. "It's the hills. Look!"

For as long as they both could remember, Mama and Uncle Graham had told them stories of their childhood. Many of these stories Mama and Uncle Graham had heard from their own father, who was one of the slaves who had sought refuge from his master long ago in those Kentucky hills. Lorraine didn't understand what a "master" was.

"Tennessee is nothing like Chicago," Lorraine's mother said. And it wasn't. The trip was more like a look into another world. Mama was kissed and hugged wherever they went; she was greeted with cries of, "Nannie! Hey, Nannie Perry's back!"

There were visits on porches with people who lavished them with lemonade and cupcakes and said, "Here's Nannie's girls and Graham's girl. Now aren't they nice!"

They met Uncle George, the uncle who had stayed behind to farm when his sister and brothers went north. It was the first time Lorraine and Shauneille had seen a real farm, with cows and hogs and a horse. Uncle George threw a burlap bag across the horse and helped Lorraine and Shauneille up. The girls clung, wide-eyed with excitement, until the horse moved suddenly, and Shauneille fell off. "Well, they're city girls, that's for sure!" laughed Uncle George, as he helped Shauneille up.

But city girl or not, Lorraine knew that someday she would like to live in a place with space and trees and lovely rich land like that.

The links between Africa and her own people became a major theme in the plays of Lorraine Hansberry. Three African brothers (Earle Hyman, James Earl Jones, and Harold Scott) confront their changing world in a scene from the Broadway production of *Les Blancs*.

CHAPTER FOUR

As she grew older, Lorraine learned of roots even deeper than those in Columbia, Tennessee. The racial pride stressed by her parents was evident in the conversations about Africa at large family gatherings, particularly at Christmas, which was spent alternately at Shauneille's house or hers. As she grew older, Lorraine's awareness of her links with that distant, exotic continent grew.

Late on one of those Christmas mornings, Mamie burst into her room and exclaimed, "Lorraine, get away from that mirror and come help me! Honestly, if you haven't got your nose in a book, you're acting something out in front of the mirror. I never knew anyone who kept to herself so much!"

Lorraine laughed guiltily and followed her older sister outside. Mamie was still the same, despite the years she had spent away at Howard University. Home just a few days, she had plunged into a round of visits with an endless number of friends, while at the same time taking part in the preparations for Christmas Day dinner.

Today, the house was filled with wonderful scents. As Lorraine hurried from room to room, keeping up with her mother's

and Mamie's directions, she inhaled soapy smells, the fragrance of fresh greens, and pervading everything, the delicious aroma of the turkey roasting in an extra-large pan, turned sideways to fit into the oven.

For weeks they had been getting ready. The house was shining. Starched curtains puffed out from the windows. The rugs, just beaten, had been turned and laid back down on the newly waxed floors. Lorraine had replaced the crocheted pieces on the arms of the chairs and sofas. When Mamie came home, they polished the silver together and washed the extra glasses that were kept on the top shelf of the cupboard.

"Mamie, have we set enough places?" asked Lorraine doubtfully. The dining room table had its extra leaves in, and every inch along the edges was set. Still, she thought of all the aunts and uncles...

But there were enough places, and everyone had plenty to eat. It seemed that her mother always had enough food no matter how many people came.

Aunt Pearl and Uncle Graham arrived first. Lorraine and Shauneille opened packages containing identical pink angora sweaters and single-strand pearl necklaces that their mothers had bought on a shopping trip together.

"That was just what I wanted!" both girls exclaimed, as they opened their presents.

Uncle Leo Hansberry came later, with his family and two African students. Lorraine smiled when she saw him. William Leo Hansberry was professor of African history at Howard

Lorraine's uncle, William Leo Hansberry, was a Howard University professor and distinguished scholar of African history. Hansberry College at the University of Nigeria was named in his honor.

University. Every year, there were at least a few young men from Africa attending his classes at the University in Washington, D. C. Her uncle enjoyed bringing them home so they could spend some time on the South Side of Chicago and learn what that part of America was really like.

"You can't understand America unless you know what its large industrial northern cities are like," he often said.

Lorraine loved listening to the precise, somewhat accented speech of these formal young men. They talked about the long, noble history of the faraway continent that had been home to black Americans before they were wrenched away and set down in an alien land.

Talk among the grown-ups on that Christmas Day covered many topics and reflected the diverse interests of the members of this big, happy family. Uncle Horace Fitchett, Mr. Hans-

Perry Hansberry, Lorraine's brother.

berry's brother-in-law, was a professor of sociology at Howard. He saw events in relation to contemporary trends, while Uncle Leo had a historical perspective. The insights of a politician were evident in the remarks of Uncle Graham, who was a lawyer and later an alderman. Lorraine's father reflected a businessman's point of view. Conversation was lively and sometimes heated.

On that Christmas Day, 1944, World War II was uppermost in everyone's mind. Lorraine's brother Carl was in the service, but Perry refused to serve in a segregated army and was contesting his draft notice.

There was a discussion of how the war would affect the racial problem in the United States, and as usual, a difference of opinion emerged. One uncle believed that the fine showing of black troops would gain sympathy for their need to be treated as equals. Lorraine's father was not so sure.

"The war's been on for three years and our troops are still segregated. I know that there's talk of changing that, but the truth is, nothing's been done about it! Enormous efforts are needed to bring black people into the mainstream of society, but there is a terrible resistance to it. Just look at Chicago! Our fight against the restrictive covenants in the Supreme Court was four years ago. Did it make a real change? What do you think? More neighborhoods are open to our people, but the fact is that Chicago is just as black and white as ever before. The politicians downtown are concerned only with the interests of the white property owners. They don't try to make this city a decent place for all."

The truth of Carl Hansberry's words was heavy on them all. His brother-in-law nodded in agreement. "You certainly know the problem, perhaps better than us all, Carl. I remember my sister standing in the doorway of a restaurant that would not serve the two of you, while you went for the police. Not very long ago, either, if I remember correctly."

"Right! And you know, Graham, there are still restaurants in this city where she'd have to do that because she wouldn't be served. And that's the mother of a United States serviceman!"

The African students listened to all of this attentively.

"You Afro-Americans do not seem to have the kind of access to the political strongholds of your country that would make it possible to protect your interests," one of them observed accurately. "Now, in my country, although we are under British rule, our people fill positions of leadership in government. Our

dream is independence. It will come, and when it does, we will be ready to rule ourselves. That is what you must do. You must become involved in the workings of government."

Lorraine listened to these young men, thrilled by their assurance and racial pride. Some day, she believed, American blacks would have that kind of involvement in the political process.

But she had noticed that lately her father seemed less hopeful about the prospects of improvement in the condition of black people in Chicago. Chicago housing was as racially segregated as it had been before the favorable ruling in the Hansberry case in the Supreme Court. The black belt had merely enlarged, he believed, to accommodate the influx of workers from the south who had come as Chicago's wartime industry had expanded.

Lorraine herself felt hurt that her brother Carl, in the uniform of the United States, was fighting for his country in a racially segregated unit. It was not until later, after the war ended, that United States forces would be integrated.

There was no disagreement with the intent young men from Africa. Lorraine's family was involved in politics and government to the extent that it was possible for black people in Chicago at that time. Both her father and mother were active in the Republican party, the party of Lincoln, and her father had served as United States Marshall and run for Congress. Her Uncle Graham, Shauneille's father, was Assistant Attorney General for the State of Illinois.

They were acutely aware of a reality that escaped many Americans at the time. Although it had been more than eighty years since the Emancipation Proclamation, many restrictions, in fact and in law, still hampered the full freedom of those Americans who had once been slaves.

As Lorraine absorbed these lessons of American history in her home, she knew that one day she would find a way to participate in the process of change that would be necessary before black people in America could become truly free. She still was not sure what form the participation would take, but she had begun to think that writing might be her way.

In later years, Lorraine marches on an NAACP student picket line against racial and religious discrimination.

Left: Englewood High School graduation.
Below left: One of Lorraine's watercolors.
Below right: Lorraine's sister, Mamie.

CHAPTER FIVE

Later that night, when the guests had finally left and Lorraine and Mamie were finishing up the last of the dishes, they had a chance to talk for the first time since Mamie's trip home.

"Mama told me you won a prize for an essay at school, Lorraine," Mamie remarked. "What was it about?"

Lorraine felt a glow of pleasure at her sister's interest. "It was about football," she said shyly.

"Football!" Mamie gasped in astonishment. "You don't know anything about football, Lorraine. You never even go to the games!"

Lorraine laughed. "You're right about that. What a waste of time they are! Sitting around outside, freezing, on a Saturday afternoon! But I didn't have to do that. I had other sources of information," she said, impishly.

Puzzled at first, Mamie suddenly remembered the unusual amount of attention that Lorraine had given her friends when she was home at Thanksgiving.

"So that's what all those conversations were about that ended when I came in! You were pumping Jewell and the boys for information for your report. Well, Lorraine, you must have

gone about it in the right way if you won a prize. Do you like to write? You've always been so good at drawing."

"Like you," the younger girl said, acknowledging her sister's ability to do everything, it seemed, in a superior way.

"But I do like to write," Lorraine continued, returning to her usual serious way of answering every question. "I think I'm going to take journalism in college," she said at last.

Again Mamie was surprised. "Journalism," she repeated, thinking it over. "Hmmm. That's a good field. Very competitive. But, as Daddy would say, 'You're a Hansberry and you're equal to it.' We should find out whether Howard University has a journalism program, Lorraine."

Lorraine took a deep breath, before she continued. "I'm not going to Howard, Mamie. The University of Wisconsin has a super journalism program and that's where I want to go."

Mamie laughed again. "Lorraine, you're growing up. You're full of surprises today. So you aren't going to follow the family tradition and go to Howard. Do Mother and Daddy know? I think they'll be disappointed."

"I haven't mentioned it to anyone but you, Mamie. And Shauneille, of course. There's lots of time yet. But when I do, I want you to help me."

Mamie nodded. "Of course I'll help, if you're sure that's what you want. But Lorraine, think it over very carefully before you decide. You know, we've both been to integrated schools and know what it's like to feel left out of things. Especially in high school, social things just weren't open to me. That's one

reason why I chose Howard. It's a relief not to fight the race thing all the time. The only prejudice in classes at Howard is against those who don't do the work."

"I've been thinking about all that, and I think I can handle it," Lorraine said, and then she couldn't help laughing. "Mamie, how can you say you were left out of things? Mama says you went to more dances and parties in high school than any two people. I never seem to really get into all that school spirit, dance and party jazz. Wisconsin will be fine for me."

Two drawings by Lorraine at college. Left: *Lynching,* depicting one of the many thousands of black men murdered by mobs in the first half of this century. Right: *Black Madonna.*

CHAPTER SIX

When Lorraine was ready for college, in January, 1948, she was still firm in her choice of the University of Wisconsin. Other things had changed, however. Her father, who had become increasingly pessimistic about his dream of equal housing in Chicago, bought a home in Mexico City, to which he and his wife planned to retire. On a vacation there in 1945, Mr. Hansberry had a stroke and died.

Mamie married, and she and her brothers, with Mrs. Hansberry's guidance, directed her father's real estate business. It was Mrs. Hansberry who helped Lorraine with her admission to Wisconsin. The guidance counselor at Lorraine's high school was surprised that she intended to go to college, and dubious about her chances of being admitted to the University of Wisconsin. Black students were not expected to go to college, nor were they encouraged to do so. Mrs. Hansberry made it clear that higher education was a tradition in their family. She pointed out that Lorraine's high school grades were so good that she should have no trouble being accepted at Wisconsin.

Opposite: Lorraine as a freshmen at the University of Wisconsin in Madison.

Perry and Mamie drove Lorraine to the Madison campus and helped her to find housing. She could not get into a dormitory, but moved into an off-campus residence.

At Langdon Manor, Lorraine lived with other out-of-state students. Several were midwestern farm girls, while others came from eastern cities. There were two Oriental students and a girl from Australia.

Lorraine made friends with a diverse group of young people at the University, including some politically radical students. She was active in the 1948 presidential campaign, but drifted away from politics when it was over.

The University was bewildering. Its bigness was something special to deal with. Lorraine had not clearly defined her own goals. She was interested in journalism, but also in art. The courses that the college required freshmen to take in order to ensure a well-rounded education seemed completely unrelated to what she wanted to learn. Math and science were the most difficult for her.

One day, as she was trying desperately to make sense of her notes in physical geography, her roommate rushed in, dropping her books noisily.

Lorraine frowned. "Where's the fire?" she asked.

"There's a play at the theater. Aren't you going?"

"Can't. Have to study. What is it, anyway?"

"I forget. Something Irish, I think."

Sean O'Casey. Lorraine remembered reading the notice. She'd been mildly interested at the time. No, she decided, being

firm with herself, she couldn't go. If she failed this test tomorrow, she'd flunk the course.

The other girl dashed out. "Lorraine," she called back, "I've got to run. I'm meeting the other kids. If you change your mind, catch up with us."

Lorraine shook her head decisively, resisting the temptation. But when she tried to return to her notes she found that she'd lost her concentration.

Finally, she closed the book. This is just a waste of time, she thought. I'll go to the play and if it isn't any good, I'll come back. The change will do me good. Even if I stay, I can study when it's over. I might be able to catch up with the others if I hurry.

But no one was in sight as she reached the modern theater building. Lorraine hurried in and took an aisle seat down in front just as the play began. Physical geography was forgotten for the next three hours as she sat spellbound while the extraordinary qualities of a number of very ordinary human beings were revealed.

Lorraine had never before been so affected by a drama. It reminded her of Shakespeare, because the people seemed so real. But they were not Elizabethans; they were contemporary Dubliners. O'Casey was a master playwright who could relate the truth about his characters in such a way that she knew their fears and weaknesses as well as their strength and nobility. The intensity of their lives was made clear in the heightened moments of his drama. What a joy to be able to do that!

But when the shimmering experience was over, Lorraine thought about her more immediate goal of learning to become a journalist. As each day passed, she felt no closer to it. It was not just the failure in physical geography. There was so little at college that she could make sense of.

When she began to think seriously about leaving the University, she called Mamie. "Do you think Mama would be upset if I didn't graduate?" she asked her sister.

"I don't know, Lorraine," Mamie replied. "But if you're unhappy, why don't you come home? Mama would understand that you want to think things over and be sure about what you're doing. I'll get her driver to take me up there to get you."

But the answer wasn't at home, Lorraine soon realized. She was unable to imagine a role for herself in Chicago. She was just as bookish as ever. Not long after she got home, she approached Mamie for help once more.

"Mamie, can you do me a favor? Mama gave me money to buy a suit and I went to the library instead. Before I realized it, all the stores were closed. I hate to waste time shopping. Would you pick something out for me?"

Mamie couldn't help laughing. "Lorraine, you'll never change. For a girl who looks as great as you do, I've never known one with so little interest in clothes. Sure, I'll get something for you. It's a good thing you like my taste!"

Lorraine sometimes wished she could be more interested in clothes and having a good time. Life would be much simpler, she imagined.

Opposite: A self-portrait on a newspaper, done by Lorraine when she was a college student.

"I really want to write, Mama," Lorraine said one day. "And the only way I'll do it is by writing. I want to go to New York. At the New School for Social Research there you can study only what you need to learn to do your work. I could take journalism courses and skip all that math and science that's supposed to make you well rounded. And we know people there, so I won't be completely alone. Maybe I'll even work on a newspaper. During the election campaign, I met someone at Wisconsin who told me about a small political paper where I might get a job."

Mrs. Hansberry was more open to the idea than Lorraine had expected. Although Carl, Perry, and Mamie had strong roots in Chicago and never expressed a desire to leave, she knew that Lorraine was different. Sensitive and serious, she seemed to be groping to find a way to express her fine potential.

She knew that the family business was of no interest to Lorraine. Why not let her try to find her way?

With the usual motherly warnings, she sent her daughter off. Friends who had been contacted helped Lorraine find a place to live. At the New School for Social Research, she signed up for a writing workshop, and she became a reporter with the newspaper she had been told about. Lorraine's political interests were budding, and on the newspaper, which expressed radical views, she began to put the black experience into a new perspective.

Not long after she was settled in the city, Lorraine applied for a job at *Freedom,* the newspaper published by Paul Robeson, the great singer and black activist, who was also a friend of the family's. For a time, she wrote for both papers.

CHAPTER SEVEN

Through her new job at *Freedom,* Lorraine became deeply involved in the lives of the black people of New York. She met leaders in the community who were trying to improve conditions in Harlem, and she attended meetings and rallies to support their efforts.

Louis E. Burnham, the editor of *Freedom,* was a poetic man with a gigantic love for people. He questioned Lorraine about her plans, and with his encouragement she began to think about a writing career beyond the limits of newspaper reporting. While she continued to report events in spare, journalistic style, her mind recorded all her experiences. She first observed them directly and then filtered them through her conversations with Burnham.

Letters home were filled with news of her new life and new friends. A name that recurred with increasing frequency was that of Bob Nemiroff, a student at New York University, who was active in the progressive movement. His parents owned a small Russian restaurant in Greenwich Village. With Bob's friends Burt and Art D'Lugoff, Lorraine began to spend many evenings at the restaurant and at other Village meeting places.

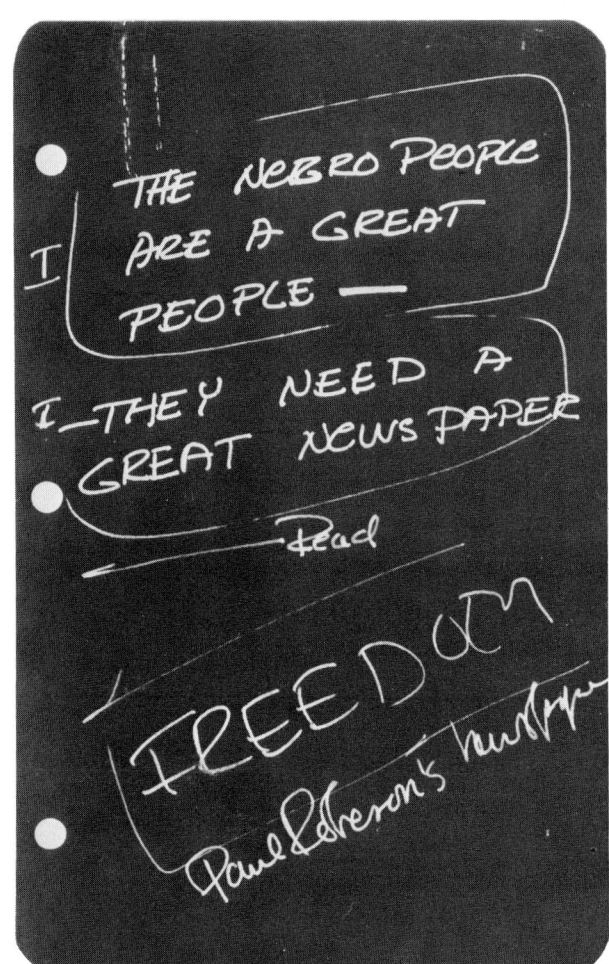

Left: A page from Lorraine's notebook written during her days at *Freedom*. "The Negro people are a great people—they need a great newspaper. Read *Freedom*, Paul Robeson's newspaper." Above: Editor and friend, Louis Burnham. Below: Snapshots of Lorraine at the *Freedom* office. Opposite page: A family gathering, 1954. Mrs. Hansberry is at the head of the table; Lorraine and Mamie are on either side of her. Lorraine's brothers, Carl and Perry, are in the left foreground.

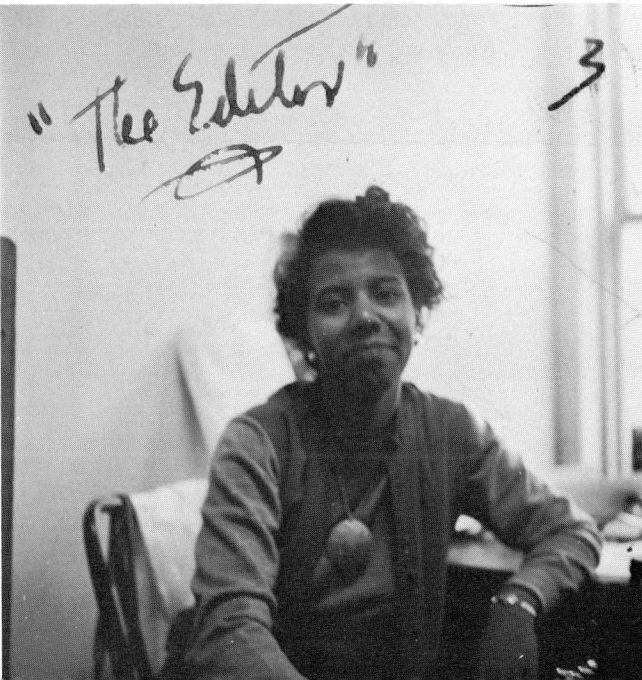

When Lorraine went home for Christmas in 1952, Mrs. Hansberry saw a marked change in her daughter. For Lorraine, this visit was different from her other trips back home. She was restless and moody, sometimes exhilarated and sometimes lonely and dejected. Her life in New York seemed too far away. She thought of calling Bob Nemiroff, but wrote a letter instead, then tore it up and wrote another one. When she was leaving, her mother said, with a twinkle in her eye, "The next time you come home, Lorraine, you'd better bring that young man with you. I've never seen you like this!"

"You know, Mama, that's a good idea!" agreed Lorraine, happy now because it would be just a few hours before she would see Bob again. "I think I'll do just that!"

Lorraine Hansberry and Bob Nemiroff were married in June of 1953. Right: About to cut the cake. Below: The bride and groom are surrounded by family and friends. Back row, left to right: Lorraine's brother Perry and his wife Carrie, Bob's brother Leo, his mother Mae, Burt D'Lugoff, and a family friend. In the front on the floor are Juanita Hansberry and Mamie Hansberry Mitchell.

Lorraine and Robert Nemiroff were married in Chicago the following June. Mamie and Mrs. Hansberry helped with the arrangements and it was a beautiful wedding. Bob's family and friends came from New York and all the Hansberrys gathered to see the Reverend Archibald Carey perform the ceremony.

After their marriage, Bob continued his graduate work in literature at NYU while he and Lorraine worked. The apartment they found on Bleeker Street in Greenwich Village had a real fireplace, lots of bookshelves, and room for a desk.

Lorraine's serious writing was taking up more of her time. She wrote only occasional pieces now for *Freedom.* Work was a succession of jobs taken to pay the bills. During the next three years, she was a salesgirl, a typist, and a furrier's assistant. She changed jobs either to earn more money or to have more hours to write. One offer, as production secretary for a Broadway play, she thought would provide an entree into the world of the theater. Disappointed when her chief responsibility turned out to be getting the coffee, she quit.

The Nemiroffs' circle of friends included other Village people, young men and women from Harlem, and Bob's old friends, Burt and Art D'Lugoff. Life was not all work. There were many distractions, some serious and some fun. Bob and Lorraine continued their active support of radical causes. At gatherings in their apartment, Bob played the guitar while their friends sang folk songs. Burt D'Lugoff was interested in folk music and asked Bob to collaborate with him on a song-writing project. The result, "Cindy, Oh Cindy," was a big hit in the

summer of 1956, and it brought a welcome change to the Nemiroffs' lives. Bob was offered a job with music publisher Phil Rose and for the first time since their marriage, they were comfortable enough for Lorraine to devote full time to writing. The luxury of having enough time was almost dizzying. She worked at the same time on a novel, several plays, and an opera.

Increasingly, one play began to take up more of her time and attention. One weekend, she realized that she had the idea for a genuine, contemporary drama.

"I want to tell the story of a real black family, and show all the complicated emotions they experience as human beings, plus the particular stress that they must deal with because of being black in America. No—even more specific than that—of being black and living on the South Side of Chicago!"

"Honey, if anyone can write that story, you sure can," her husband encouraged her. "Are you thinking of a family like yours?"

Lorraine shook her head slowly. "Not really," she replied thoughtfully. "We weren't typical enough, Bob, because of my father's education and his real estate business. He put himself through college, you know, at a time when few people had a college education. And he was a successful businessman. We were really comfortable, with nice clothes and household help.

"There was one thing about being black—no matter how well off you were in Chicago in the 1930s when I was growing up, you lived in the black section of town. So I've known lots of people like the family in my play.

Lorraine on the roof of the Bleeker Street apartment.

"This family will be involved in a struggle. I want to show people who have to worry about money, but who have aspirations to a better life. There are so many courageous people like that in the ghettos. Life gives them a rough time every day, and yet they manage to survive. When there's a chance to assert themselves, they seize it.

"That's the problem I'd like to pose in my play. You see, poor people living in a ghetto don't have the opportunity to make too many choices that could change their lives.

"Usually, they must accept what life offers them—an apartment in a particular section of town, and a certain type of job. But that doesn't mean they're happy with it, or that they don't have dreams of acquiring something better, if not for themselves, then certainly for their children."

"And you want to offer them the opportunity to make a choice? About what?" asked Bob, curiously.

"Well, think how it would be if a family like that suddenly came into some money—say from an insurance policy—enough money to make a rather big change in their lives. Think of how each member of the family would have an idea about how to spend that money. I'll assume that they'd all be interested in improving their lives—I don't mean that someone would just want to gamble it away, or spend it foolishly—but I'd be able to show the conflicting values that exist in a family."

"Have you thought about the things they might choose?"

"Yes," Lorraine answered thoughtfully. "A strong mother would choose education first of all, and then I think she'd want

a nice place to live. The surprise in her choice would be the fact that she'd be willing to risk a lot to live in a neighborhood that was cleaner and safer, even if it was hostile at first.

"If they considered moving out of the black section of Chicago, they'd have to contend with a neighborhood associations's hostility, the way my family did when my father made that choice years ago.

"The grown-up members of the family might have other values that would determine their choices. Perhaps one of them would be agreeable to the idea of spending the money for education, but would reject other values of the mother. This person could introduce ideas of liberation or assertiveness. Another person would want to invest the money in a business venture so that he could be his own boss. For him this would become just the first of many choices. The play would need someone who could see merit in all of these choices and could clarify the conflicts."

"Would you tell the story like that?" Bob asked her.

"It needs a dramatic incident to create a clash in the values, some crucial element to pose the whole problem and then create a resolution of it. What I want to show is that the people in a family like this aren't all alike. They have complicated emotions and a yearning for a comfortable way of life. That's a very American approach to life—the desire for material things. Added to this would be something more that black people bring to American life—a strength acquired by having survived generations of struggle and suffering. Their history as a people

One of Lorraine's favorite spots in the apartment was the floor in front of the fireplace. Here she sips a cup of coffee as she starts a new book.

gives them the courage to confront difficulties with affirmation, rather than with despair. Also, there's a struggle between members of different generations—the confrontation of traditional and nontraditional values."

As she and Bob talked, the idea for the play became more sharply focused. That weekend, Lorraine shut herself in the bedroom and worked steadily at her little white desk. By Sunday night, she had completed the first act.

She was exhilarated. Of all the projects that she had worked on, this one was becoming the most dominant in her thoughts. Bob was excited when she read it to him. Lorraine had created genuine individuals with unique conflicts. Her story of a rather ordinary family named Younger, who lived on the South Side of Chicago some time after World War II, was believable, humorous, and appealing. The mother's aspirations and the conflicting values of her grown children and grandchildren were evident in Lorraine's skillful writing.

"Honey it's good, really good. What are you going to call it?"

"Remember Langston's poem about the crystal stair?" Lorraine began to quote one of their favorite poets, Langston Hughes. It was a poem about a black mother who labored to enable her son to live a better life. "I'm thinking of calling my play *The Crystal Stair.*"

"I love it!" exclaimed Bob. "It's perfect. If you can sustain the kind of tension that you've created in this first act, you've got something good here. I always knew you were great!"

But there were many problems to work out before the play was completed. Lorraine worked on the manuscript for many months after that.

Self-portrait: "Nameless, faceless."

CHAPTER EIGHT

One afternoon, nearly a year later, Lorraine pulled the last page of her manuscript from the typewriter and added it to the neat stack of typed pages. The room was dim with late afternoon shadows, but she did not switch on the light. Instead, she rose from the desk and went into the living room. Stretching out full length on the floor in front of the fireplace, she lay face down on her folded arms, thinking about the play she had just completed.

The first act was almost exactly the way she had originally written it. Writing and rewriting the remaining two acts and shaping the story into an entity had taken the better part of the last year. At some point in the writing, she began to concentrate on another Langston Hughes image, of a dream that is not realized, drying up like "a raisin in the sun." It became the focus of her imagination and the title of her play.

What would happen to her play now, she had no idea. Later, her husband would be home, and he would read the entire

Opposite: Lorraine enjoyed playing the guitar during moments of relaxation.

manuscript, as he had read each completed scene. He would be the first person she would share it with. For just these next few hours, it would belong only to her.

The Younger family created in her imagination was a combination of qualities found in countless numbers of people Lorraine had known. In the daughter, Beneatha, there was something of Lorraine herself as she had been years before, a teenager alternately fearless and questioning. In the elder Mrs. Younger, there was a little of Lorraine's perception of her own mother, blended with that of all the indomitable mothers she'd known in Chicago and Harlem. Her brother Perry's dynamic personality emerged in Walter Lee Younger, the son. Lorraine shaped this character into an individual with the drive to be successful in terms of acquiring money and respect. Mamie's personable ways were evident in his wife, Ruth. Boys like their small son Travis had skipped their way through all the black neighborhoods she'd walked in. He was the little brother she'd never had. More than that, he was the hope of each generation—the child who would reap the benefits of hard work and sacrifice and make them bearable.

It was important to Lorraine to report accurately the truth of what she had known in her life. She wondered whether those who read it would recognize that truth.

She knew Bob would like it. He was a never-wavering source of love, strength, and appreciation. He read it later the same day, straight through. Alternately reading it aloud and silently, he savored the lines he liked best. At the end, he whistled softly.

"Lorraine, it's good. Maybe great!" he said with admiration. "You've managed to write something that has the essence of pure drama. In a brief span of time, you've revealed a sense of the lifetime conflicts of this family in such a way that their experience seems universal.

"Although your play is about one specific family at a clearly defined time of their lives, there is so much truth in their experience that the reality of their situation would seem familiar to others.

"What are you going to do with it now?"

Lorraine was thoughtful for a moment. "Bobby, would you believe that I've hardly thought beyond this moment of writing the whole play? But I'd like to have someone else read it, someone like Burt or Phil, or Phil's wife. Do you think they would?"

"Doris is away on tour, I know, but why not ask Phil? And Burt, too. Maybe they haven't had dinner yet. Think you can stretch the spaghetti and meatballs?"

Lorraine jumped up. "You call them, and I'll get busy. After all this solitary work, I'd love a party!"

Burt D'Lugoff, Bob's old friend since their college days, and Phil Rose, his boss at the music company, arrived an hour later. Lorraine doubled the sauce and spaghetti and set the rosewood dining table with straw mats while Bob went around the corner for candles, Italian bread, and red wine. In the company of old friends gathered for a celebration, dinner was satisfying and fun.

After the dishes were cleared, Lorraine brought out the manuscript and they settled in the living room. She clowned at

Another one of Lorraine's self-portraits. This one, *Clown*, seems almost intended to serve as a reminder not to take herself too seriously.

first, posing in front of the green fireplace wall and insisting on proper audience behavior before she began to improvise a comical introduction. Catching her spirit, Burt and Phil clapped, stamped their feet, and whistled, demanding that she begin.

For the next three hours, Lorraine read the play aloud. When she finished, Burt's reaction was much like Bob's. His enthusiasm and admiration were sincere. He and Phil discussed the characters and actions with Lorraine, asking questions about background and movement, trying to imagine the play as they might experience it in a theater.

Lorraine was thrilled. It was a joy to hear their reactions. What had been until then a private endeavor, they treated seriously and intelligently. They were talking about the play not just as

something written by a dear friend but the way they would speak about a professional work. The evening ended with them urging Lorraine to get her play produced.

"Acting groups here in the Village are always looking for good new material," insisted Burt.

"Burt's right," agreed Bob. "That's the next thing to do. You want to hear real actors read this, Lorraine. Let's try something like that."

"When Doris gets back from her tour, I'd like her to hear it. She may have some contacts that you could try," said Phil Rose, referring to his actress wife.

When they were alone again, Lorraine remarked to Bob that Phil's response to the play seemed more subdued than Burt's.

"Well, he's really not in the theater, Lorraine. Music is his field. But you could tell he really liked it. He's just not as expressive as Burt."

Although Phil Rose had had no direct experience as a theatrical producer, he took a giant step in that direction the next morning when he dialed the Nemiroffs' number.

Lorraine listened to Phil for a long time before she called Bob to the phone. With a stunned look, she handed him the receiver. "Bob, talk to Phil, please. He just said the most incredible thing to me."

She sat down in the living room, holding the typed manuscript against her chest, unable to believe what she had just heard. When Bob returned, she could see that he shared her feeling of astonishment.

"Bob, why would Phil want to produce my play? And on Broadway! I didn't know he was interested in being a producer."

"He never has been, Lorraine. I'm as surprised as you are. Aside from Doris's acting, I've never heard him mention it. But it's a genuine offer. He said he's having a contract drawn up, didn't he?"

"Yes, he did. Bob, I'm embarrassed. I didn't ask him here expecting him to produce my play!"

Bob laughed and hugged her. "Phil knows that, honey," he assured her. "And he isn't doing this completely out of friendship, either. Remember that Phil is a businessman and he invests in something of value. You'd better get used to it, Lorraine. You've written a real play that's going to be produced on Broadway! Now all you have to find out is how that happens."

"Bob, I haven't the faintest idea about how something like this becomes a play that people see in a theater, do you?" she asked, waving the manuscript that she was holding.

"Nope, and you know what I think? Neither does Phil! But he has contacts with people who do know about it, or he wouldn't get into this. He is a very capable guy and does a good job with anything he gets into."

Broadway, in New York City, is the heart of the American theater. On Manhattan's West Side the theater district begins at Times Square and continues north to Columbus Circle. All the better-known theaters are in this area, and during any season a playgoer has his choice of fifteen or twenty plays to see. Although the best American plays have not always opened

there, it is the place professional theater people think of as *the* place for a play to be. Reviews of Broadway plays are reported via the wire services to cities across the country. Plays that are Broadway successes usually tour the country on the strength of the good reviews they receive from New York critics. In the months to come, Lorraine, Bob, and Phil had a crash course in theater production.

While Lorraine continued to rewrite and polish her play, Phil Rose approached the well-known Broadway producers, asking each one in turn to join him as co-producer. He was not successful. The play was very different, they said, from plays that were usually seen on Broadway. They failed to see the complexity of the human values that were examined in the story and questioned whether theater audiences would have any interest in a play about a black family. It was true that there was no precedent for Lorraine's play. When black characters appeared in Broadway dramas, they were usually cast in minor or demeaning roles, or those that had little effect on the action of the play. Black performers were known primarily for stereotyped or comic roles or for roles in musical plays.

Not long after the contract was drawn up, Phil sent the script to Sidney Poitier to read. Poitier was an actor known for six or eight good movie roles. He had the strong personal qualities that would make him ideal to play the role of Walter Lee Younger. He was enthusiastic about the play, and recommended Lloyd Richards, his teacher, as director. When they met Lloyd, both Lorraine and Phil were impressed with him.

"Phil, do you realize what a milestone this production will be?" Lorraine asked one day. "A black director has never worked on a Broadway play before."

"I realize it only too well, Lorraine," Phil replied ruefully. "We're running into all kinds of difficulties. At first, financial backing was our big problem. Now that we've solved that by finding a large number of people to invest fairly small sums of money, we're encountering other obstacles. The major hurdle now is to find a theater."

"I don't understand," said Lorraine, puzzled.

"Theater owners are reluctant to book a play unless there's some assurance that it will be a good solid hit. They look for signs of what they call 'commercial success.' "

"Like a musical comedy?" she asked.

"Exactly. Like a musical, a surefire hit, the kind of thing that's loaded with big names who've been associated with other successful plays. You know what I mean—music by a well-known team, sing-along songs, a great cast, and so on. Or a comedy," he continued. "Even a drama will do, if it has a nice, easy, noncontroversial theme. Theater owners like to sign long-term leases. With a hit show that sells tickets long in advance, a theater owner can relax, knowing the theater will be occupied for a full season or more. On the other hand, if he rents the theater to a production that closes after only a few performances, his theater may be left vacant for the remainder of that season. They're cautious men, but you can appreciate their reasons."

"Phil, I'm nervous," Lorraine shivered. "So many people have invested money in this. What can we do?"

"Continue along the way we have been," he replied with calm assurance. "We'll keep trying to book a theater and, in the meantime, we'll put the show into rehearsal. Finding space to rehearse will be no problem. I believe in *A Raisin In The Sun,* Lorraine. It isn't going to let anyone down!"

It was only later that Lorraine and Bob realized the risk Phil Rose was taking. Once the show was in rehearsal, it was like being on a moving train. Rehearsal salaries are lower than the regular salaries paid to actors after a show opens, when the play is earning money. The actors' union permits rehearsal salaries to be paid for only four weeks. After that, it is necessary to pay the regular salaries, even if the show doesn't open right away. This makes a considerable difference in expenses. In addition, contracts are drawn up with costume and set designers, with additional investments and obligations. As each week of rehearsals passed without the promise of a theater to bring the play into, the situation became more serious.

While Phil continued his efforts to book a theater, he made arrangements to take the show out of town for tryouts, first to New Haven, Connecticut and later, to Philadelphia, Pennsylvania. Out-of-town tryouts give the cast experience before an audience, without the pressure that exists in New York. Based on the out-of-town experience, changes are often made in plays before they open in New York. Rarely does a producer plan these performances, however, until he has a Broadway theater

rented and waiting. As each day passed, the situation became more critical. Characteristically, the resourceful Phil Rose chose a creative alternative.

When Bob arrived in Philadelphia in time for the last rehearsal, Lorraine could see from his expression that he'd heard the latest news.

"Bobby, what do you think of taking the show to Chicago before opening in New York? I'm wildly excited about it opening first in my home town, but at the same time . . ." Lorraine's voice trailed off in bewilderment.

"It sounds like a good idea to me," Bob replied thoughtfully. "Representatives of the Shubert chain of theaters were impressed with the New Haven reviews and they've offered the Ethel Barrymore Theater as soon as it's empty in March. Moving the show to Chicago for a month will have it paying its way. And the chain is willing to share the transportation costs."

Lorraine shook her head in wonder. "Phil and his associates are really professional, Bob. I've been able to stay clear of management problems and concentrate on the play." Lorraine interupted herself to point suddenly to the stage.

"Look at Lloyd, Bob. Watch how he does this!" Bob saw the director halt a scene in rehearsal and call aside Ruby Dee, who played Walter Lee Younger's wife, Ruth. After some softly spoken comments to which Ruby listened intently, he signaled the other actors in the scene to redo it. Ruby's emphasis on several lines shifted only slightly, but there was a perceptible difference in the smoothness of her delivery.

In the hotel during the New Haven opening of *A Raisin in the Sun.*

Lorraine chuckled softly. "Lloyd is fantastic. I don't know what he says when he stops a scene that way and gives those private directions, but whatever it is, it works."

The distraction over, she turned to her husband again. "Bobby, I'm scared," she confided. "So much is involved, so many people have demonstrated their faith in my play. Suppose it's a bust?"

"Lorraine, it can't miss! We know there are enough playgoers who will recognize its value. This is a great human drama, Lorraine, in the finest tradition of American and European contemporary theater. It's right up there with the best of them—all your heroes. You've talked about learning so much from Sean O'Casey. This is a play that he could understand and love. As soon as it opens, its quality will be apparent to everyone. Remember, won't you, that I said it first?"

Poster and scenes from Broadway's "Best Play of 1959," *A Raisin in the Sun*. Above right: The Younger family looks on as Mama (Claudia MacNeil) opens her gift. Below left: Walter Lee (Sydney Poitier) laughs with his son, Travis (Glynn Turman). Below right: In another scene from the Broadway production, Ruth (Ruby Dee) looks on as Beneatha (Diana Sands) does an African folk dance.

CHAPTER NINE

On the evening of March 11, 1959, Lorraine Hansberry took a deep breath as she made a last check of herself in the mirror. Her sister Mamie, in New York with Mrs. Hansberry for the opening night, recommended Lorraine's simple but stylish black dress and suggested the long rope of pearls to wear with it. Win or lose with the New York critics, at least I'll look elegant, Lorraine thought.

The last months were a kaleidoscope of images in her mind. She regretted that she hadn't written down more of these experiences, because she knew they would never be repeated in quite the same way.

Miraculously, everything had worked at the New Haven opening. No director's nightmares materialized—collapsing scenery or flu-striken cast members. Good reviews from that trial run had made tonight's New York opening possible.

Lorraine's most cherished memory of New Haven would surely be the chambermaid who came into their hotel room late in the week, when she and Bob were packing to go home. At first the chambermaid started to leave, apologizing for intruding. Then she stopped, and asked hesitantly, with an Irish

brogue accenting her speech, "You're the author of that new play, aren't you?"

Lorraine beamed. She was becoming accustomed to hearing herself addressed as the author, but was still enjoying it enormously.

"Yes, I am. Did you see the play?" she asked hopefully.

"That I did! And a wonderful play it was!" replied the maid with an intensity that surprised Lorraine. "How did you manage to know those poor people's problems so well, Miss? That Mrs. Younger was so real, she might have been my own mother. Your play reminds me of the best of the Irish writers."

No praise was quite so thrilling. "You can't imagine what your words mean to me," Lorraine said softly. "My inspiration was an Irish writer, Sean O'Casey. He is a giant among dramatists and if you see some small relationship to his tradition in my work, it is a tremendous compliment to me."

The Philadelphia opening was an exciting event because of the large number of black people in the audience. A friend of Lorraine's, himself an author and playwright, told her that he'd never seen so many black people in a theater before. Later, they crowded about her outside the stage door, where she stood autographing their programs until the very last one went home.

The Chicago opening was special for a number of reasons. Although she was publicly embraced as the successful hometown girl, there was an undercurrent of uneasiness about the arrival of the play. In fact, Carl and Perry tried to persuade Phil Rose not to open the show in Chicago. With Mamie, her

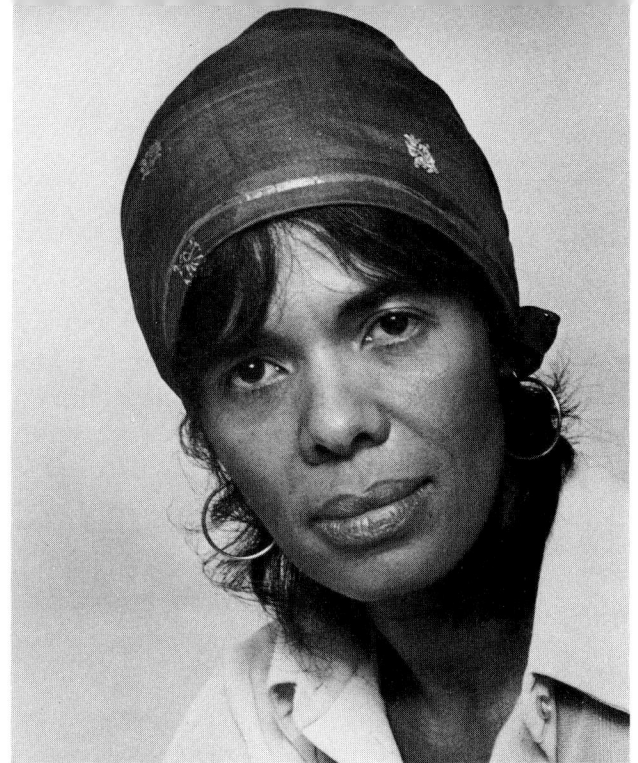

Lorraine's cousin and childhood friend, Shauneille, came to the Chicago opening of *A Raisin in the Sun.*

brothers managed the Hansberry real estate business. Their efforts to make good housing available for all people, like those of their father earlier, were still resisted. The hostility that they encountered from various pressure groups in the city made them fearful that the play would not be treated fairly in the press.

Phil Rose considered the risks, and correctly decided that enough favorable publicity had preceded the play from its New Haven and Philadelphia runs to make real difficulty unlikely.

In addition to the public red carpet of welcome for Lorraine, there was the opportunity to share this moment of triumph with family and old friends. Their pride and her joy seemed boundless. Best of all, Shauneille was there with her husband. Shauneille, who like Lorraine had been shy and intense as a child, was now a talented writer and actress.

Although the play opened with good comments from the Chicago critics and enthusiasm from the audiences, Lorraine was still nervous on the night of the New York opening. Too many shows opened out of town and flopped in New York. This first night would determine whether *A Raisin In The Sun* would settle down for a good long run, or close quietly. The New York critics, she knew, held the key to her play's future. If they liked it, they would go home tonight and write favorable reviews. Playgoers would read those reviews tomorrow morning and head for the box office, if they liked what they read. The advance sale of tickets would stimulate more ticket buyers to call. The most cherished possessions of New Yorkers are tickets for a play that is sold out months in advance. Some will buy tickets for only such shows, figuring they have to be good if so many people want to see them.

So, it was yet another gamble. She and Bob were quiet on the ride uptown to the Ethel Barrymore Theater. Earlier that week, after the signs were first hung, they'd come to take pictures. Tonight the theater entrance was ablaze with lights and the lobby crowded with playgoers dressed for a special occasion.

The next few hours were a rapid succession of impressions. The supercharged atmosphere before the curtain rose gave way to tremendous exhilaration at the first intermission. All Lorraine could remember afterward were collage-like images of smiling faces. Mamie told her later that a man she recognized as one of the drama critics stopped to speak with her and Mrs. Hansberry as they made their way up the aisle. Not knowing

who they were, he asked what they thought of the play. Mamie told of how she laughingly explained why she had a certain bias in its favor. The play was beautifully acted. Once the curtain went up, the emotional impact with which Lorraine hoped to transmit her ideas to the audience was the sole responsibility of the actors. She sighed with contentment as the curtain descended after the second act. They had surely picked the finest actors for this play. Sidney Poitier was a marvel of timing and of controlled emotion, while Claudia MacNeil, in the part of the mother, had the kind of resonant voice that exuded authority. As Walter Lee's wife, Ruby Dee was warm and appealing, yet torn by conflict. Diana Sands had just the right amount of adolescent energy and verve. It worked! Incredibly, it was as she had imagined it long ago. No, it was even better than what she had imagined, because it embodied the creativity of all of those who became involved as it took shape.

As the final curtain came down and the actors appeared to take their bows, the audience was on its feet, cheering. One curtain call followed another in a tremendous ovation. Lorraine watched with joy as the actors came out again and again to acknowledge the applause. They deserved every bit of it, she believed. And then, unexpectedly, Sidney Poitier leaped from the stage, caught her by the hand, and pulled her up beside them to share in the acclaim!

Afterward, there was the cast party, a mingling of congratulations with a touch of apprehension, as they all waited for the early editions of the morning papers to appear with the reviews

CROSSWORD PUZZLE
Edited by MARGARET FARRAR

ACROSS
1 Radar warning signal.
5 Part of 10 Down's name.
10 Tent furnishings.
14 Puerto ——.
15 Between: Fr.
16 Distinctive air.
17 Title from Langston Hughes poem.
20 Locked cellaret, named after mythical king.
21 Go —— (deteriorate).
22 Particular.
23 Entreaty.
24 Harangue.
27 Man's name.
31 Fruit.
32 Con —— (with spirit): Mus.
33 Tribe of Israel.
34 Vestment.
35 New York city.
36 Son of Gad.
37 Longshoremen's group: Abbr.
38 Hair wave: Colloq.
39 Neckerchief.
41 What N. B. means.
44 Member of sect in India.
45 Goldman aggregation.
46 Chemical combining form.
47 Art exhibitions.
50 Exact opposite.
54 Attribute ascribed to Cornelius Melody.
56 Shop- ——.
57 "—— Ben Jonson."
58 First name in the Cabinet.
59 Hied.
60 To stop: Span.
61 Be at ease.

DOWN
1 Impudent child.
2 Coin of Italy.
3 "—— get it for you wholesale."
4 Star of 17 Across.
5 Plastered.
6 Per ——.
7 "—— never too late to mend."
8 Vase with foot or pedestal.
9 Agree.
10 Creator of the Julian calendar.
11 River in northern England.
12 Correct.
13 Substance for castle-building.
18 Fills fully.
19 Did field work.
23 Last king of Troy.
24 Where Toledo is.
25 Musical instrument.
26 Seaport of Morocco.
27 Jacques, for one.
28 Notions.
29 Roulette bet on four numbers.
30 Piece of flat silver.
32 Mingle.
35 One concern of labor unions.
39 Maugham character.
40 Come a —— (fall headlong).
42 Teem.
43 Bench: Fr.
44 Commodition.
46 Within: Prefix.
47 Pulls alternately, as on reins: Colloq.
48 Over.
49 Learning.
50 At a distance.
51 Seep.
52 Origins: Abbr.
53 Coup d' ——.
55 Pray: Lat.

6-13-59

One certain indication of success—inclusion in the widely worked *New York Times* crossword puzzle. This was sent to Lorraine by a friend. In the margin Lorraine wrote: ARRIVAL!

and confirm the audience's reaction. At last the newspapers arrived, and there was a general feeling of relaxation as they were read. Both the *New York Times* and the *Herald-Tribune,* the first papers to appear on the stands, and the most influential of the metropolitan dailies, reviewed the play favorably.

Lorraine's first success was a triumph in many ways. As successful playwrights go, she was extremely young to have a play produced on Broadway. Women were rare in the field, and black women nonexistent.

The next day began a period of a kind of activity that Lorraine had never known before. She was the talk of the town, and everyone wanted to see her, hear her, and photograph her.

Requests for interviews and radio and television appearances poured in. She enjoyed every minute of it. She and Bob accepted invitations to parties for months afterward. Each day, the mail brought a special reward. Letters came from people who were moved to express their appreciation. She was grateful to them for sharing their experiences with her, and she attempted to answer every letter.

The months slipped by quickly. With the first excitement beginning to fade a bit, Lorraine could schedule a little work each week on writing projects that had been set aside for the past year. Then, in May, the New York Drama Critics voted *A Raisin In The Sun* the best play of the year. Another triumph and more attention for the first black person—and the youngest American playwright—to receive the award!

Later, when a movie was to be made of the play, Lorraine adapted her script for the screen. It, too, won public acclaim and critical accolades. More than ever, she was in demand by the media.

When she began to speak on topics that were dear to her, Lorraine was very articulate. Her natural shyness vanished and her warmth and intelligence emerged. These personal qualities made her a popular radio and television guest. Speaking engagements were hard for her to refuse, particularly when they came from groups with which she felt a special affinity. But all of this took time from her serious writing. At last she found herself wanting to shut off the phone and get away to a quiet place to work.

She and Bob purchased a house among the lovely hills that rise above the Hudson River in Croton, New York. It had the quiet, green space that she had promised herself long ago when she visited her mother's birthplace in Columbia, Tennessee.

Lorraine divided her time between writing in Croton-on-Hudson and supporting the civil rights movement and the peace movement. She was frequently called upon as a well-known and articulate spokeswoman for the black cause.

Times were changing, particularly for the young people who came up from the South to explain their nonviolent attempts to do away with racial discrimination in public places. In addition to her personal appearances in their behalf, Lorraine and Bob helped these earnest young men and women by raising funds for them.

Burt D'Lugoff and Bob sought help from people in the entertainment field. They organized a committee, which included several of the student leaders who were relatively unknown in the North, and arranged a series of concerts featuring popular artists to raise money in behalf of the civil rights movement.

In Croton, the Nemiroffs held a meeting to explain the cause to their neighbors and ask for their help. Judy Collins, the popular singer, sang a new, evocative song by Bob Dylan and the crowd joined in with chorus after chorus of "Blowing in the Wind." Afterward, people from the meeting gathered at the Nemiroffs' house for a cookout. The money raised that day bought a station wagon that took three young students from the North who wanted to help the black people in Mississippi. The

When Bob and Lorraine moved to their new home in Croton, New York, the first thing Lorraine did was nail up this "Chitterling Heights" sign on one of the trees.
Below: A sketch Lorraine did of the Croton property and Lorraine herself sitting on a bridge as she relaxes on a summer day.

Lorraine spent much of her time in the civil rights struggle. Left: At an NAACP rally with singer Dave Sears. Above right: At Croton after a fund-raising meeting for voter registration in the South. Right: Lorraine and husband, Bob. Below left: Poster for the Broadway production of *Les Blancs*. Below right: Lorraine, Theodore Bikel, Nina Simone, SNCC chairman John Lewis, and others at a 1963 SNCC meeting.

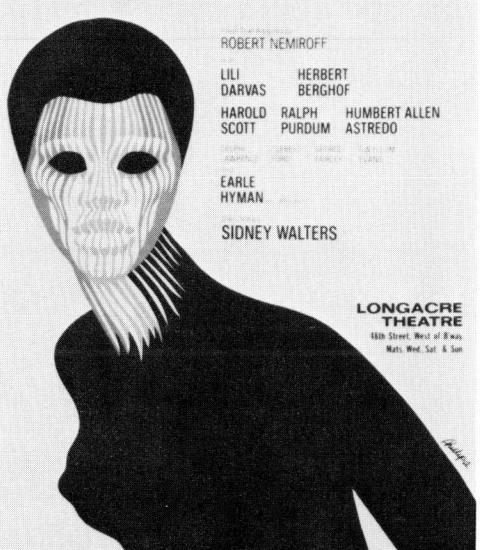

three men never returned, and their murders created outcries of shame and rage throughout the country. It was no longer possible to ignore the inhuman things that were happening.

Lorraine never sidestepped the moral issues that were at the heart of the struggle for civil rights. No opponent was too big or too powerful for her. When she believed they were mistaken in their judgments, she took them on, from the editorial board of the *New York Times* to the Attorney General of the United States. Now and then, surprise was expressed at the ferocity of her responses. Many who did not know Lorraine's deep moral convictions, and judged her solely on her cheery television personality, were startled by her unyielding stand against injustice.

While she never completely left the arena of the struggle, she continued her commitment to a decision she had made long before. More than ten years earlier, when she left the staff of *Freedom,* Lorraine had consciously given up much of her day-to-day direct involvement in the civil rights cause and decided to use her talent as a writer. Her statement would be made artistically, rather than primarily through direct action.

To this end, she worked on several projects at once. Among these was the libretto for an opera based on the life of the Haitian revolutionary Toussaint L'Ouverture; *Les Blancs,* a dramatic affirmation of the African liberation movement; and a television script called *The Drinking Gourd,* finished but never produced, that was a stunning indictment of the evil of slavery.

The success of *A Raisin in the Sun* led to *Raisin*, a musical version of the play, which won the 1975 Tony Award for Best Musical of the Year. Above right: *Raisin* stars Joe Morton (Walter Lee), Ralph Carter (Travis), Ernestine Jackson (Ruth), Virginia Capers (Lena), and Deborah Allen (Beneatha) pose together. Below: A scene from *The Sign in Sidney Brustein's Window*, starring Rita Moreno and Gabriel Dell, on the right.

CHAPTER TEN

The years after the success of *A Raisin In The Sun* brought personal sorrow as well as happiness to Lorraine. The problems that her family had in Chicago at last became overwhelming, and they gave up the real estate business, left the city, and settled in Los Angeles.

Difficulties occurred in the Nemiroff marriage. Lorraine and Bob decided to separate and in 1964 were divorced. Professionally however, they remained in close association. Lorraine still relied on Bob as a friend, critic, and advisor.

In the same way that *A Raisin In The Sun* had penetrated her consciousness, another play was beginning to form in the forefront of Lorraine's imagination. It was the story of an idealist who became involved in a political campaign. Sidney Brustein rose above the mediocre circumstances of his life to commit himself to the belief that people can be better than they are. *The Sign in Sidney Brustein's Window* was based on many truths about people that Lorraine had learned from her friends in Greenwich Village. Once again, the idea of ordinary people revealing extraordinary emotions posed a dramatic problem for her to bring to the stage.

As usual, she worked simultaneously on another project, the narrative for a book called *The Movement: Documentary of a Struggle for Equality*. This was a book of photos for SNCC (Student Nonviolent Coordinating Committee), a civil rights organization that had conducted the sit-ins in the South.

Writing the new play became a struggle for the young woman in a way that she could not have anticipated. Always aware of the fleeting nature of time, she felt an urgency now to finish her work. Odd, seemingly unrelated, physical symptoms had been troubling her for some time. After a number of examinations, it was thought that she had an ulcer, and she was operated on. Later, there was a visit to a famous clinic and another operation. Lorraine was seriously ill, and for about a year she alternated periods of productive work with stays in the hospital. The need to use time wisely was added to her natural compulsion to write.

When the play *Sidney* was written, there was no difficulty in gaining financial backing or a Broadway theater, as there had been with the first play. What an entree a well-known name was!

Bob Nemiroff and his old friend Burt D'Lugoff became producers and arranged to open the play at the Longacre Theater in New York. Very weak when rehearsals began, Lorraine moved into a midtown hotel with a nurse in order to maintain close contact with the play. She forced herself to resolve artistic dilemmas despite constant pain. Bob and Burt, unable to help her, wrestled with the problems of production.

On October 15, 1964, *The Sign in Sidney Brustein's Window* opened at the Longacre Theater. Lorraine came to the theater in

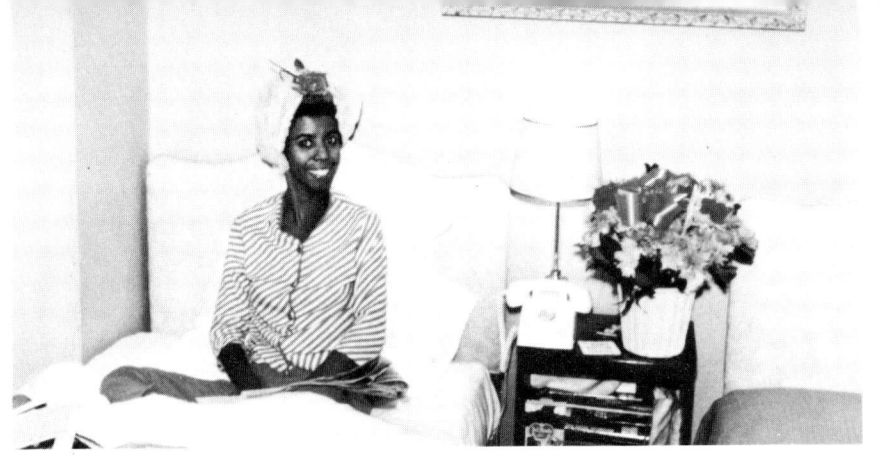

When rehearsals for *The Sign in Sidney Brustein's Window* began, Lorraine moved into a midtown hotel with a nurse. By this time she was very ill, but wanted to maintain close contact with the play.

a wheelchair and took a seat near the back. She stayed for a short time after the curtain came down to greet friends, and then went back to the Hotel Victoria. She was weak and tired, but tremendously moved by the performance.

During the play, Bob Nemiroff thought with heartbreak of the beautiful, courageous woman who had succeeded in creating a number of wholly believable, troubled human beings who found hope for their future. Although her characters could have chosen to ignore the problems of life, they preferred, as she did, to challenge and overcome them instead. Not liking the world he lived in, Sidney Brustein tried to change it for the better.

In a telegram to Lorraine that night, Bob reaffirmed his belief that *The Sign in Sidney Brustein's Window* was in the tradition of great plays that celebrate ordinary people and to which audiences actively respond.

The drama critics did not agree with him. The next day, Bob and Burt brought Lorraine the bad news of the newspaper reviews. It was almost certain that the play would have to close.

Not enough tickets had been sold to keep it open even for a week. When people read the reviews that morning, no lines would form at the box office. It would require about $20,000 of income each week in order to keep the play open, and they could not imagine a ticket sale that would come even close to that figure.

While they discussed these melancholy financial facts, a phone call came from two colleagues who believed in the play and offered them $2,500. It was the beginning of a surge of support from other theater professionals who saw the play's merits and pledged time and money to keep it open. They were acutely aware of the problems involved in bringing serious dramas to Broadway, and the importance such plays had in vital, living American theater. Actors and actresses called friends and urged them to see the play. Others spoke to groups that normally buy blocks of tickets for theater parties. Religious leaders who recognized the moral and spiritual questions addressed by the play talked about it in their churches and temples. In the months to come, always the time of the year when plays are the least well attended, hundreds of people joined together to keep the play running. It was an incredible story of repeated closing notices that were canceled by a swelling of new support.

Meanwhile, Lorraine's physical condition grew worse. On the Saturday after opening night, she made an urgent telephone call to the theater, and Burt D'Lugoff, who was a doctor, rushed her to the hospital. Three days later, she lost consciousness. Lorraine had cancer, and there was little hope for her recovery. Her

doctors believed that she would not last the day. After four days in a coma, however, she regained consciousness and, gradually, her strength. At first, she could see a little, and before long she was able to speak and eat. Lorraine knew that she was seriously ill, but she never relinquished hope that she would live and return to her work. The intensity with which she lived all her days glowed within her to the end. In the following two months, she was able to embrace the outpouring of caring and loving that was keeping her play alive.

Lorraine Hansberry died of cancer on January 12, 1965. She was thirty-four years old. At her funeral services, in a Harlem church among the black people whose courage she had so often saluted, her family and friends gathered to celebrate her life. Her friends from the theater and the civil rights movement drew from Lorraine's own words to reaffirm her belief in people.

Lorraine's will bequeathed her literary work to the care of Bob Nemiroff. After her death, when he began to go through her papers, he was astounded to find so much there. In Lorraine's years of writing, she had accumulated a large body of serious work that was as yet unpublished. In addition, there were letters, diaries, and interviews that together were an explicit statement of the philosophy implicit in her fiction.

One of the first tasks Bob set for himself was an artistic arrangement of this collective statement with excerpts from Lorraine's imaginative work. When it was organized into a work for the stage, he gave it the title *To Be Young, Gifted and Black.*

These words were also Lorraine's own, taken from a speech that she had given in May, 1964, commending the winners of a writing contest sponsored by the United Negro College Fund. Leaving the hospital to keep the speaking engagement, she urged these young black writers to write about the world, not only as it was, but as they thought it ought to be. Later, he completed the almost-finished play, *Les Blancs,* and had it published in a single volume with the draft of another play, and a completed television script.

Meanwhile, two young men who wrote music and had been captivated by the lyrical quality of *A Raisin In The Sun* when they first saw it, contacted him. Their discussions developed into the musical adaptation, *Raisin,* which Nemiroff produced. Winner of the 1975 Tony award for Best Musical of the Year, *Raisin* completed a long, successful Broadway run and then toured the country.

Once more, the words of the young woman who saw so clearly the possibilities for greatness in even the frailest of human beings rang out. The melody of life that she first sang is hummed now by a new generation of playgoers. The texts of *A Raisin In The Sun, The Sign in Sidney Brustein's Window,* and *Les Blancs* are included in literature courses of study in high schools and colleges. On many college campuses, students have been intrigued by the depth of the writer's experiences explored in the dramatization, *To Be Young, Gifted and Black.*

Lorraine Hansberry found a way to express her faith as an artist in words that would transcend her brief lifetime.

One of the first things Bob Nemiroff (above) did after Lorraine's death was arrange much of her material, most of it unpublished, into a work for the stage, *To Be Young, Gifted and Black*. The original Off-Broadway cast included those below, left to right: John Beal, Janet League, Andre Womble, Cicely Tyson, and Gertrude Jeanette.

BIBLIOGRAPHY

Atkinson, Brooks, *New York Times.* 3/12/59, 27:1-2.
Atkinson, Brooks, *New York Times,* 3/29/59. II, 1:1.
Baldwin, James, Sweet Lorraine. (Introduction) in Hansberry, *To Be Young, Gifted and Black,* 1970.
Drake, St. Clair & Cayton, Horace, R, *Black Metropolis: A Study of Negro Life in a Northern City,* (Rev. ed.) New York: Harper & Row, 1962. 2 vols.
Hansberry, Lorraine, *A Raisin in the Sun* & *A Sign in Sidney Brustein's Window.* New York: Signet, New American Library, 1966.
Hansberry, Lorraine, *To Be Young, Gifted and Black.* adapted by Robert Nemiroff. New York: Signet, New American Library, 1970.
Hughes, Langston, *Montage of a Dream Deffered.* Holt, 1961.
Kerr, *New York Herald Tribune.* 3/12/59.
Nemiroff, Robert. (ed.) *Les Blancs: The Collected Last Plays of Lorraine Hansberry.* New York: Random House, 1972.
Nemiroff, Robert, *The 101 Final Performances of Sidney Brustein.* (in Hansberry, 1966.)
New York Times, 3/13/59. 25:3.
New York Times. 1/13/65.
New York Times. 1/15/65.
New York Times. 1/29/65.
New Yorker, 1959, 35:34.
Vogue, 1959. 133:78.
Shimmy Shimmy Coke-Ca-Pop. A Collection of City Childrens' Street Games and Rhymes by J. Langstoff and Carol Langstoff. Doubleday, Garden City, 1973.

ABOUT THE AUTHOR

Catherine Scheader was born in New York City where she studied English literature and art at Hunter College and taught elementary school. After a move to Monmouth County, New Jersey with her husband and three children, Mrs. Scheader attended graduate school at Rutgers University and began to write biographies for young people. Her first published series of books, *Proud Heritage,* told the stories of five notable Black Americans. Mrs. Scheader has also written fiction for children. Her own children, Barbara, John, and Susan, read all her manuscripts and offer suggestions. Mrs. Scheader's husband is a deputy chief engineer with the Department of Water Resources in New York City. Mrs. Scheader is a reading specialist in the Marlboro Township public schools in New Jersey.